Educational Adviser: Lynda Snowdon
Designer: Julian Holland
Picture researcher: Stella Martin
Artist for Contents pages: Julian Holland

Photo credits:
J. Allan Cash, 6-7, 10-11; Aspect Picture
Library, 18-19; Alan Hutchison Library, 4-9,
12-13, 16-17, 20-21, 24-31; ZEFA, 14-15, 22-23
Cover picture: Alan Hutchison Library

Dillon Press, Inc., 242 Portland Avenue South
Minneapolis, Minnesota 55415

This edition published by Dillon Press by arrangement
with Macmillan Children's Books, London, England.
© Macmillan Publishers Limited, 1983

Library of Congress Cataloging-in-Publication Data

Steele, Philip.
  Festivals around the world.

  (International picture library)
  Summary: Text and photographs describe festivals
from all over the world, including a bun festival in
Hong Kong and a parade in West Germany.
    1. Festivals — Juvenile literature.   [1. Festivals]
I. Title.   II. Series.
GT3933.S72   1986   394.2'6   86-2023
ISBN 0-87518-332-8

International Picture Library

Festivals Around the World

Philip Steele

DILLON PRESS, INC.
Minneapolis, Minnesota 55415

Contents

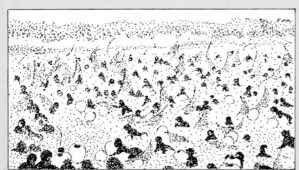

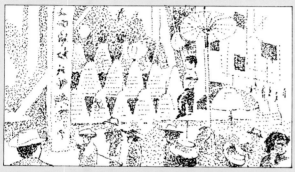

Dogon Dancers in West Africa (Important Days)
These dancers are Dogon people, from Mali in
West Africa. They are wearing skirts made of straw
and wooden masks. The masks are often made to

4

look like animals such as dogs and lizards. The
Dogons dance on important days of the year.
They have a special dance to thank the gods for a
good harvest.

Fishing Festival in Nigeria (February)

Every February there is a fishing festival at Argungu in Nigeria. Hundreds of fishermen jump into the river. They carry nets to catch the fish. There is a

competition to catch the most fish. The best fishermen win all sorts of prizes. There are also prizes presented for swimming, diving and canoeing.

Sallah in Nigeria (According to Islamic Calendar)

If you are a Moslem, you are not supposed to eat during the daytime for one whole month every year. You eat between sunset and dawn instead.

This month is called Ramadan. When it is over, there is a big festival. This festival is called Sallah. At Maiduguri in Nigeria, people beat drums and there is a big parade.

Good Friday in Malta (Friday before Easter)

These Christians are carrying statues through the streets. The statues tell the story of Jesus dying on the Cross. The people are in Mosta, on the island of

Malta. Every year on Good Friday they have a
procession. They walk to the cathedral in the town,
dressed in grey or white robes. Then they celebrate
Easter with a special church service.

Morris Dancers in England (Pentecost, May Day)
These are Morris men. They have bells on their feet
which jingle when they stamp their feet and dance.
In their hands they carry sticks or handkerchiefs.

They use these when they dance. They also wear
special costumes. You can see them in England
at Whitsun (Pentecost, seventh Sunday after Easter)
or on Mayday, as well as at other times of the year.

Carnival in West Germany (Before Lent)

Here come the clowns! It is carnival time in
Germany. There are fancy dress parties and
parades. The clowns are leading a colorful parade

through the town of Rottweil. The fun lasts for several days. The last day of the carnival is Shrove Tuesday, or Mardi Gras. This is the day before Lent (the 40 weekdays before Easter) begins.

15

Sun Festival in Peru (June 24)

Long ago, a people called the Incas lived in the town of Cuzco in Peru. They believed the sun was a god called Inti. They worshipped this god. Today,

the people of Peru have a festival to remember the Incas. On June 24 every year they watch the sun rise at this old fortress. They wear Inca costumes when they celebrate this festival.

Chinese New Year in San Francisco, USA (Jan./Feb.)

Many Chinese people live in the USA. They like to enjoy their New Year in the old Chinese way. They carry a beautiful paper dragon through the streets.

Wherever the dragon goes it brings peace and good luck. The people also set off firecrackers. These are meant to scare away evil spirits. The festival goes on into the night.

Bun Festival in Hong Kong (May)

Everybody likes eating buns, but these buns are special ones. They are supposed to bring you good luck if you eat them. This is the Cheong Chau

festival. It happens every year in Hong Kong. Food is important in many other festivals as well. For instance, in Britain, hot cross buns are eaten on Good Friday.

21

Harvest Festival in Japan (October)

These men live in Japan. They wear wooden masks and carry drums. They are dancing at a men-furyo or masked festival. They dance for the harvest.

They also dance for the rains that make the crops grow every year. They beat the drums as they dance and shake their heads. The festival takes place every October and lasts three days.

Ganesh Chaturthi in India (August/September)
This festival is held in the city of Bombay in India.
People are carrying the statue of Ganesh down to
the sea. Ganesh is a Hindu god. His statue has the

24

head of an elephant. He is a very popular god. When people have problems, they ask Ganesh to help them. They believe that he can help them solve their difficulties.

Procession in Sri Lanka (August)
Every year, people in Sri Lanka bring elephants into the town of Kandy. They cover the elephants with brightly colored cloth. The elephants walk in a

grand procession through the streets. There is music and dancing. This is a Buddhist festival which goes on for ten days. Men and women dance in the streets by torchlight.

Water Festival in Burma (April 17)

Would you like to splash water all over your friends? Then you should go to Mandalay in Burma on New Year's Day! On that day the Buddhists of

Burma go to their temples. After the ceremony in
the temple, the fun begins. At this water festival
nobody can keep dry for long. These young girls
look very happy and wet.

Horse Festival in Indonesia (April)

This horse festival is taking place on the island of Sumba, Indonesia. The island is famous for its

horses and riders. Long ago, fierce warlords ruled

over the island. Today, it is much more peaceful,
but there is a festival instead. The riders hold
pretend battles and remember the warlords. They
also give displays of horse riding.

Places Featured in this Book

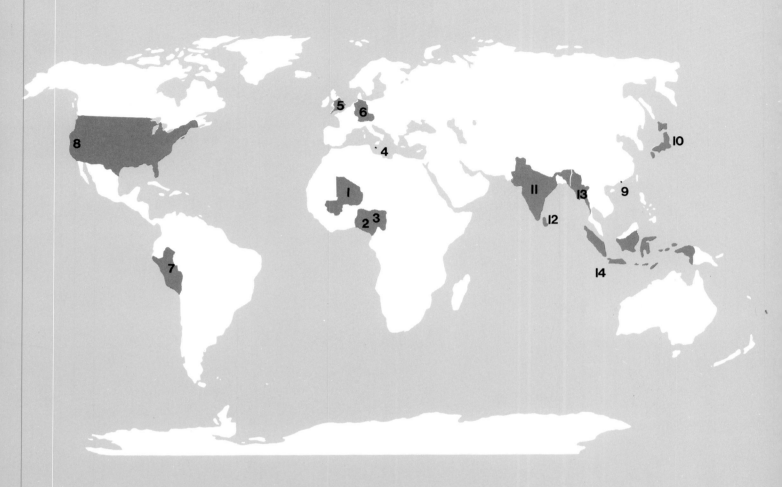

1	Dogon Dancing, West Africa	**8**	Chinese New Year, San Francisco, USA
2	Fishing, Nigeria	**9**	Bun Festival, Hong Kong
3	Sallah, Nigeria	**10**	Harvest Festival, Japan
4	Good Friday, Malta	**11**	Ganesh Chaturthi, India
5	Morris Dancing, England	**12**	Procession, Sri Lanka
6	Carnival, West Germany	**13**	Water Festival, Burma
7	Sun Festival, Peru	**14**	Horse Festival, Indonesia